A Bus Trip Is Fun

T0020339

EMERGENCY EXIT

AATKings

166

AAT KINGS COACH COMPANY PTY LTD
ALEXANDRIA
Acc. No. 11853

SCANIA

Saving Our Planet

I am going on a bus.

I will be on the bus for a long, long time.

Here is my seat.

I can see a long,
long way.

I can see the **hills**.

I can see the **beach**.

I can play a **game**.

A bus trip is fun!

beach

game

hills